Hard Reds

Brandi Homan

Shearsman Books
Exeter

First published in the United Kingdom in 2008 by
Shearsman Books Ltd
58 Velwell Road
Exeter EX4 4LD

www.shearsman.com

ISBN 978-1-905700-81-3

Cover: 'Logan Square #4': photograph by Ursula Sokolowska, copyright ©
2008, Ursula Sokolowska.

Contents

III. The Valentine Factory

Hard Reds

For my parents,
who taught me to take risks,
and Aunt Jackie,
a writer in her own right.

I

LIKE THE DEVIL

Explaining Poetry on a First Date

Is like telling the Prom King why I'm in Chess Club
but still want the corsage, the one with the tiny basketball.

Why I can name every Tri-state poet, but don't know local DJs.
A Pilot pen makes me happier than any red satin

dress with polyester loofah sleeves. All my friends
carry Moleskines. One scrawls homophones on her hand,

another taped a pencil to his headboard. We collect epigraphs,
read out loud in empty rooms. There's a library in my bed.

How do you explain wanting to die or marry yourself?
That success isn't a matching loveseat or the Whitesnake video?

I don't want to get my picture taken and leave the dance early
because my head's full of streamers and cardboard stars.

The lights are always low. It's affliction not religion.
Not once have I thought I could be saved.

ECHOLOCATION

I pulse now, once:
I want a man who can
build me new planets
out of mint and tin and
still maintain good posture.
One with bare feet
and big hands that carry
lavender in wheelbarrows
through my yard.
Hands that hammock.

I bump and swell.
A man with a wingspan
from Gombe to Galveston,
who folds me
into knotted shoulders,
all thumbs and metacarpal,
like a papoose to backboard.
Stiff as my high school
boyfriend's letterman jacket—
thick with forget-me-not.

A man who doesn't care
I'm only in love
with his overbite.

The tare between maxilla
and mandible. How his
zipper snags my lip—
He doesn't give a shit
that I'm seduced by violet.
I love the way his hair will smell
twelve days from Sunday.

Terminal buzz: I want a man
who'll never stand
for terra firma, who dangles
by his toes for the wind
alone. One who comes out
swinging. I'll soak his scars
in coconut milk, I'll heal him
with heliotrope. I'll grow
sanguinaria in my navel,
throw clover from the roof.

Decibels somersault
—*look back, look back*—
but lilac lands in the canyon
without an echo,
and I keep writing love songs
that vanish in thin air.
One day, he'll nose
my nape for blood.

Red Dress Cento #1

In the arithmetic of red dresses,
a red dress means go. Unlike most
vagabonds in sturdy boots and a stained
rucksack, I wear a red dress and slingbacks.

And there'll be no scream from the lady
in the red dress dancing on her own.
I had to cross the solar system
on foot before I found the first thread

of my red dress. On the night avenue
I am a brag in my red dress: *I dare you.*
It is only me, sitting in a red dress,
imbibing red drinks.

And the red dress (think about it,
redress) is all neckhole.
I put on that red dress and that is all
I ever did for poetry. A girl who sat

by oranges, wore a red dress. Sometimes
I walk though my village
in my little red dress all absorbed
in restraining myself—a woman in a red dress

is the reader's digest condensed book of love.
All my life I saved for that red dress.
The red dress crumpled like cellophane.
The red dress a wilted petal on the floor.

POEM FOR JASON RAY

A poem about you would begin with a belt buckle,
a West Texas town, a field of sweet potatoes
or peach trees that sway

that say this is how air should taste:
sasparilla, sweetgrass, foam, quarry.

It would be littered with shingles,
a lop-sided shed like a white cat
in a dark field, a weather-worn tomcat.

It would leave tools all over the house,
T-squared, weave around sawhorses.

It would be reflexive, a humor choked
with asphalt stretching like clotheslines, backseats,
the cowboy's long tendons.

It would breathe sparks, a circle of stones
itching with rusted railcars that sand

the levee of my skin, distilling it into blues:
a damp haystack, a dog's side sliced on barbed wire,
a guitar that reveres silence.

A poem about you would be in two-steps, line dances, of city
and sidewalk, the language between them, the hidden.

It would chop cedars, mine gypsum.
Be full of cinnabar dust, raw erupting knuckles
behind the bucking chute.

A litany of bathtubs and slow-leaking faucets.

LIKE THE DEVIL

He holds on to life with his teeth,
dangles it by the nape.
Tastes with the fury of cayenne
and says *hush-hush-hush*
with his hands as he drinks
wine from me like an open spoon.
He can tell magenta from maroon.
He grins like the devil,
all jump-start and red bell
pepper. Stitches me together
as if my cunt is a wound,
his tongue, copacetic.
I mend, sprout wings,
and scream things.
A firebird possessed
of the power to fly,
he shuts his eyes
and wills it so.
Off he goes.
Grunt and scruff, this
spitfire. This hellcat.
A scrapper who turns the screws
of my truss rod, straightens
my back. Names the stars
of my knees with one eye

closed, opens my gates,
faces the bull.
Olé! He's *muy caliente.*
Itch, bitch, and boil,
he celebrates supine
and sublime. Pins
the tail on the donkey
every time, this toreador.
A necromantic lynx who
swallows whole but plays
legato, in tune.
He follows me out of rooms.
Hush-hush-hush.
It will be all right.
He who holds on to life with his teeth
will never go hungry.

GARDEN RUN WILD

I slipped a thorn beneath your hoof.
Rubbed my scent, a wild cinnamon,
thyme, into your nostril with my thumb
like ointment. You're slippery,
a scent. All thumbs, nostrils, hooves.
Beneath cinnamon. Thorns caught
in my ointment, rubbing listless.
Like thyme grown wild beneath brier,
thorns. Cinnamon slipping
into my sunset, your listless thumbs
like hooves over my slip.
I'm scenery. A wild.
Thorned, you've left me hooved
and slipping in cinnamon. In thyme.

On the Quite Contrary

Call me Magdalene.
Wash your feet with my tears,
the cannabis that cleansed my hair
spiraling about your toes.

Our most distilled selves, these mirabilia.
This desire to dip in the perfume pot
of metaphysics, to subvert ourselves to ethanol.

I'm bloody.
I'm buggin'.
How to get from A to B?
Moan, map, or memory?

The tilt-and-whirl of voracious hips,
dehisced laughs and fingertips,
tattoo your truth upon my split

lip. Lick and spit.
Hiss.
I call you the name your parents denied you:
Wanderer. Fist.

With desperation, you connect my dots
from ilium to ischium, that tasty trapezoid.
As if geometry equals affection,

I cure your belly with nicotine,
and the salt lick of your tar dissolves
on my tongue, magic to molecules.
Your face so new it's faceted, bilingual.

The disco ball's shatter and splint
are never the same snowflake,
and I'm in love with your smile's punctuation:

Apostrophe and it's me you've contracted.
I'm missing letters.
How to make an alphabet with only
H-O-P-E?

I take off your glasses to see
how I've changed you. That trick
turned. My, your translucent eyes.

Seven demons excised, but oh,
the ones that were left.

SIREN

Seduction with slingbacks draped
from the V of her fingers. Brutal
lipstick, a pipe, Mama's cross
tossed down her neckline, thin
film forming between metal
and skin. Just like every male
dreams of a red-haired woman,
every female dreams of a red dress
that makes her clash from bottom
to breast, the plié of her calves
beneath carmine thighs.
False eyelashes splayed
back like rims of fly-traps,
solace leaks from her body. Skinned
knees, beauty at the blade's edge:
a jack-knifed tooth and letters tied
with black straps. We all want it—
I've stopped dyeing my roots,
started chainsmoking. Brother,
get your truck and a gun.
I'll teach you German and gin
rummy. Bite my lip and see
what color I bleed.

COUNTRY SONGS ALWAYS TELL STORIES

And loving you is like living
in a Toby Keith album, deep-throated
and baritone, barrel-chested passion making
sad things sadder. You're running all cylinders,
five hundred horses, and for the first time
in a long time (which is what I would name
my own country song), I believe
you are a bull in a china shop.
Storeowners riot like in *Beauty and the Beast*,
the giant who doesn't know his strength,
Lennie in *Of Mice and Men* who kills
the boss man's wife because he's scared.
I've always felt sorry for Lennie and giants
and you, little bull with the thousand china
cuts I would lick shut. Suddenly I find
I no longer believe in fairy tales
or fiction because I've never been a princess
who didn't know exactly in whose hands
she was placing her heart. Whose hands
had the reins. Your cuts will close,
I promise, but you will snap my neck.

MEDITATIONS ON A BALL BEARING

I spin you, cinctured by convention,
With warm beer and delphinium
Under my eyes, a need to circle
Back around. You filter

Life into threads, cradling radial
Load and thrust to reduce
Friction, to smooth sparks out
Into days graceful as bell curves,

Outer rim virulent, inner
Rim stock-still, a maverick.
Things roll better than
They slide. Slick as conceit

And shiny as conscience
In your weaned casing,
Whenever I watch you
I ache everywhere soft.

To the Tune of *Friends in Low Places*

When the visit with old friends
is over, I cry into the steel sink.
I'm in no mood
for Chicago.

My old dreams phoenix into
mercury, beautiful poison. I want
Texas this time.
Lawn. Rodeo.

Both Ends of This Road Lead to Desert

I wanted South Africa.
He said he could tell good genes
by the shape of a girl's calves,

spoke Afrikaans in the elevator.
He traced my Achilles' tendon
like a vet checking a feline spine.

I remember the world
being smaller, Texas, the two-fingered
wave. I never knew Del Rio,

drove from one mountain in Vegas
to another. Folded his directions
into a scorpion, seersucker, a solar

eclipse. I missed the turn
onto Sunset, the empty house. Nellis
a new shirt. I should see Thailand,

Tokyo. Stop succumbing to tailored pants,
buckle shoes. I've never met a man
I couldn't get a good poem from, but

both ends of this road lead to desert,
and already the world
is wide, is wide, is wide.

II

Two Kinds of Arson

Open Letter to a Crush

Here I go again,
forcing him into my love like air
into a balloon. Listen, Crush,
take back your incessant fingers,
the prodding between the curtains
of my ribs, moving my lips.
I'm no dummy.
Go ahead. Stiffen my joints,
stop my breath like a street
without a breeze. I know
hope is heresy,
so give me its collar.
His ambivalence won't keep
my neck from bleeding
when I turn my head, you heretic's
fork, you scavenger's daughter.
I do not recant.
I've forgotten how to breathe
without burning.

LOOKING FOR DESNOS

Friday night on State
and Randolph, the only good
bookstore two trains away,

I'm looking for Desnos.
He isn't here of course,
on this day of scotch

neat and penny loafers,
but I'm bored and keep looking—
Dickey, Dickinson, Dryden

too done and Eady too genius—
I fall on Flynn, Nick Flynn,
whose name is quicksilver

on the tongue, fricative
like the spark wheel's
spin that makes butane

breathe—
Steve Young and Sam
Spade, Nick Flynn.

This man, a gun, and I'm under
his blue and white cover,
inside that true crime.

I've got diastemata—
teeth rearrange
in my mouth for this,

bite through his garden
of chill and splinter.
His words in storage—

closer to brick, grout.
The darker you become,
the lighter you may be—

Angelization through ink
on paper, tool on tool.
Come bum a cigarette, Nick,

*I need your warehouse
of black rubber.* He shakes
his head, smiles at me

for luck. Nimbused,
his pretty, empty hands.

Two Kinds of Arson

—And when it was bad,
we believed maple trusses
were enough. I was a charnel

half-buried in earth—
not the clean soil of soybean
rows, but filth, the dark meat.

He'd tie my hair back in bows.
The doctors gave me naphtha
and told me it was a parade.

Sparklers swimming in slow circles,
I was in love with kerosene
from the fire breather's mouth—

how to get so much from one body?
Genetic tinderbox,
girl gone up like a match.

Bones dried in, we fingernailed
brush rakes to the wall, spackled
sinkholes. I became acolyte—

prescribed burn so hot
these letters are firebrands,
this book an empty room.

Nostalgie de la boue

Bassists strive for the low end, prefer E-string
to D, unafraid of the floor. Sending down

roots, they evangelize for distortion, squeeze
sevenths from the stompbox, walk the bass line

between roadblocks. Ghost notes, dead notes,
overtones necessary but hard to hear—timbre of blood

not pulse, that ticking watch which cinctures
our wrists. Not the practical backbeat of kettledrums

or doorbells. Not the dripping faucet. No, this tremolo
underlies every circadian rhythm that stretches

through tightrope, stridulation like a tickle
at the back of the throat. Murmur of water

under seaplane. Bottom, excrement, foundation—
the living vibrato over which cement is poured.

SHRUBBERY

I'm told to sit
still but I writhe,
try as I will.
Your brambles begin.
Thin, they grow.
Chokecherry that wriggles,
swirls. Weeds to thicket,
your honeysuckle girl.

Soon, I'm a rose garden.
Woven of pet names,
ruse, thorns that warm
from bud to bloom.
A kudzu quilt,
polychrome thatch
emitting your hues
that quiver, catch:

Presto! I'm white.
Light and linen,
you are mine.
Peel the bandages back
to pass the time, if you must.
Inside, I'm dust.
I glitter, I glow.

COHABITATION

How to fall out of love
with one who deters locusts,
whose name is a heartbeat
in my mouth—a man
who leaves me begging for a rib.
He leans over, whispers,
It's yours, you know,
my light. Eat swiftly.
I bite and come away
neon. Wiping my tongue
with my thumb, I taste
the problem of onomatology,
one fruit both mango and radish,
the shape of the thing to do.
No matter, it's all pith,
and bradycardia begins
its soft, slow hiss.
Sooner or later, my teeth
would crave blood, our lungs
licked to bedstraw.
How smoothly we slip
through this field of poppies
where plagues go to die,
crawling on elbows
through the long, crisp stems.

RED DRESS CENTO #2

You're a little bluejay in a red dress
on a sad night. Drink, and let my hand
open your red dress, my mouth consent
to its good fever. Do I say this life is beautiful

and dangerous, a red dress soaked in gasoline?
Too often, you wake up holding the phone
in a tight red dress. You never arrived splendid
in your red dress without trouble for me

somewhere, somehow. Take your red dress,
leave the hanger. Here's a picture
of where you live, your street,
your red dress. A loss of address.

A red dress.
This language is wealth,
a red dress, an injection—the one who left
you in your red dress and shoes, the ones

that crimped your toes. In a red dress,
you answer a telephone and say,
so sweetly, I. A throatful of gore
and a red dress. In the most elegant

store, you buy a red dress, a fan—
a pearl-handled revolver.
Baby, put your red dress on.
My hands coming down all over you,

the red, red dress,
and more hands.

THE EMPTY SIDE OF THE BED

If you must know,
when I kick you
during the night,
it's no sleep spasm.
I mean to.

I'm tired of you,
open flank,
closed prairie,
withering aster.

I'm done
with your heady
doe-eyed dream, shadow
in the shape of love's
twin: relentless rain,

a tongue that tastes
only lead. Always
a railroad crossing
with the gates down.

ODE TO THE BARYCENTER OF A BINARY STAR

Well-oiled pearl,
space spindle,
your two bodies revolve
with infinitesimal patience,
a bond bigger than blood.
How not to love stars
that circle like giant electrons
around you, nucleus, vow-
like point of force. One dot
in the center of nothing
that changes everything,
orbits reduced to geometry.
My, what a beautiful asterism.
Still, one says ascension,
the other, declension,
all those exes and ohs.
The desire for occultation
runs deep. See how they stay
so long on the same plane.

POEM IN WHICH I AM MY OWN PORN STAR

Most days I just want to live
in a Crate & Barrel catalog.
I can't stop watching *Law & Order*.

I'm losing heat and you aren't here
to absorb it. The free daily
calls this recycling program "ineffective."

You said erection and I felt health class,
CPR dummy. You took the free condoms.
I'm Artificial Annie.

There's no lifeguard on duty.
Dear High School Reunion,
Dear Pedestal Effect—

I spend a lot of time trying
to increase the space between my pinky
toe and the rest of my foot.

I am my own alien,
my own porn star.
Spectacular, stunted.

What is Occam's razor?
The best thing about a sandwich
is not the pickle next to it.

I am damaged but still quite good.

Folie à deux

I miss it—our idioglossia
for the world to wonder at,

making foreigners from natives.
Equal parts quote, neologism, night

like the one we bathed and conjured
a country from our bodies thrumming

with myocytes. O, how we ached
to become bigeminal, two heart

beats, solecistic territory.
You traced borders on my body,

majuscule script in sentences
down my legs. My words

apocopes, letters smudging off
in the water as I wrote, you

looking like a leopard,
ink bleeding out in spots.

Cursive slanted the wrong direction
in fat, round drops.

AFTER READING FENNELLY'S OPEN HOUSE

I realized "Katrina" meant Katrina
Vandenberg, the poets were friends.
Maybe once they were Jessi and I,
confessing over High Lifes at Innertown
we knew who we were dedicating
our as yet unwritten books to,
epigraphs like tulle bows on pews.
Vows without grooms, our books,
credits already bustled up in back,
colophons ex-lovers who watch
from the annex or last rows
like final pages, otherwise empty.
Printer's ornaments trembling
in the bride's hands. We know
who gets copies, inscriptions
with more thanks than any note
for bread plates, a garnish tray.
We may never own gravy boats.
            So when I think of Katrina
and Beth Ann, they're not teaching
or reading or even writing, but
in some red-lit bar with Fifties pin-ups,
drinking Jameson with back rent,
sambuca shots. They're spouting Pound,
waving cigarette circles in the air,

telling each other they're brilliant
until people look, and the bartender,
the cute one, says enough.

CENTRIPETAL FORCES

Nights at the California Clipper—
black booths, red light, no white

except Rockin' Billy's hair
as he covers "Ring of Fire"

for the late crowd, nothing
but ash looking for a good wind

to send us from this flayed world
where violence and beauty are the same

end of a bone that pokes
through skin at an unexpected

sunset, that first, best kiss.
A movie with a gun on its cover

will rent more often,
but we ignore this industrial life—

gears and rudders that got us here
without our knowing how or why—

our violence bent steel, cold-
cocked, beauty that's not white—

bordello without the tango,
the value in shoot, kill.

SELF-PORTRAIT IN BLUESHIFT

As if I have cyanosis,
indigo in my creeks and pockets,

I'm throttled with futility,
the black-throated blues.

I walk the bottom of a pool,
an aquarelle I saw

in a calendar once, ataxic,
cumbrous. Legs of rill

and tendon. Everything
transient and malleable,

ultramarine. Hips piscine, half-
open. Mouth full

of blue darners and fugue
suspended in vitro

like secret slow
bubbles. Here, light stretches,

glossal bands doubling
me in currents.

Ink, this empyrean estuary.
Hair slicing my neck in pluvial,

iridescent threads as I walk
this floor of turquoise, soporific

ruin, this bent, blue
note.

Put Your Hands on the Plow and Hold On

I know I'm in it for the long haul
when I misread a sign that says
Adopt a Pet as *Adopt a Poet*
and think I'd adopt Ed Roberson
because he appreciates this kind of thing.
Like when a friend of a friend was drunk
and said *chickened, I'm so chickened!*
When really slurring *shit-canned*.
Or my sister wanting to *ride the Eskimo*
when she meant *escalator*.
That and Ed knows everything,
like how there's no word in English
for when a woman gets excited
but in Zulu it's a navigational term
meaning *moon on the water*.
We laugh and Ed covers his mouth
like a boy, talks with his fingertip
under his nose like he's shushing.
He must see writers as rosebushes,
Gallicas in need of pruning.
When he cuts so close he loses us,
he nods and says again *Listen. Listen.*

Another Poem That Means I Miss Him

This could be a series too.
I should bring in midnight somewhere,
how the Indian guy carried me
to the patio to get a beer, the stage
like it's summer camp.

How spoiled I was.

Maureen left for the bathroom early
and never came back.

That was Monday.

For four days last week I worked
construction at Coach House in the mall.

Nina says it's fucking inappropriate,
makes me feel guilty for flirting.
Garrett says she has big labia, says I can still
hold his hand. Six years and it comes down
to dinner. If some punk kid from Lake Forest
can tie the knot, why can't I?

Once I was even on SportsCenter.

Sometimes things get too big
for me. A man who smells like
hot wings, a trope. A cooler with a radio
built right in.

MARYLAND

Which is softer: his hair
splayed over your stomach,
postdiluvian eyes

on the velvet edge
of forest, or pages
from his book, running

your fingers through letters
slipshod with sibilance,
black-eyed susans?

He flicks cigarettes
with his thumb, boxers
paper-thin as cherry

blossoms bleached
into submission.
You bend over the desk.

Sex sugared off, you're
a saucepan of molasses
boiling with elements

lost—hydrogen,
carbon. This basement
on Elizabeth Street

scented with bergamot,
you're left all aguamiel.
He named the calico Baltimore—

À bon chat, à bon rat.
It's simple semiotics.
You think *marinara,*

he thinks *Florence, August,*
a field to the brim with blackbirds.
He'll make Italian

dishes shattered
on the floor between you
into something beautiful.

To the Other Woman's Lover

Those sea stars under her jacket are miles of diamonds.

You know.

Her navel never sleeps, that ruby firework,
that clacking scallop. Lava, she boils.
Shoes coiled to flint metal against metal.
Flamenco.
The spark and grind of heels on wood,
she is neon, tango's fulcrum.

Is it possible to be this high?

This in love with gutters? Windows?
We're all bits and pieces,
the pink lick of her with more power than platinum.
Purrs with the dyskinesia of atoms, telepathy.
Riot! It is never really about men.
It is not about you.

Why I'll Never Play the Cello

It's not because I have small fingers,
pointy elbows. Or because I like to let my nails
grow long, cacophonous. I'm simply not meant
for the litany of your spruce chrysalid. Too vast,
you carmine cask, perilous barrel. If skimmed
right, I might splinter, fission into diatonic
atoms, loose chords. The circumference
of my arms too distant to be halved
by the likes of you, a secant slicing
my very circle, a knife through the body
of a pear. I've only played pizzicato, clumsy
with tenor in a Winn-Dixie jug band.
Some fingers defy pinning monarchs
to mounting board. They refuse calluses,
split seams, rip triplets open with a hook.
Maybe, if you were a seesaw, my hips
could bear the bass and treble, the up-
and-down, the cry and sing that ferment
in the bellies of whole notes. Or a motorcycle
between my knees, pure glissando, electric
meow. Zero to eighty in the breadth of a grace note.
Nothing but wind between here and heaven.
No, a cello is different. Burlesque. Merlot
salted with crosses and cadenza,
you're raw, rubicund. Heady

groans extorted from andante for the price
of vine. Purfling tortured with burgundy,
twisted into our own private adagio cut
from suede cocoons, the unraveling of silkworms.
These ways are easier: motorcycle, seesaw, pizzicato.
I've no room for you, cello, in this sarabande
of bleeding fingers. Feet firmly on the ground,
knees vibrato with prayer. My head somewhere
beyond bouquets and butterflies alike.

INVOCATION

Come bring me love
on open couplets. Let me taste

its tin until my teeth ache
from clinging like soft black grapes

to an otherwise fruitless vine.
Let each stanza be a plank,

a cable bridge across a gulch
which is a weak metaphor

for desperation—a cold, deep end-
stop furrowed with brittle vineyards.

I'm looking for love
exploding like walnuts

in the metal grip of sonnet.
I expect nothing less

than another line, another
rhyme, a dark and weathered seed.

III

THE VALENTINE FACTORY

ORIGINS

How strange to be named
after alcohol and a song
about a cocktail waitress

with a good ear. What's more,
a motorcycle on my birth
announcement, a powder-

puff enduro. No wonder
I have a penchant for high
heels and cheap silver,

wear t-shirts that say
I Kiss and Tell,
rings on all fingers.

I can't be held responsible
for amber in my eyes
around soft-spoken strangers,

or gasoline fumes I suspire,
the need for everything
raw and fast.

Sentient, sentimental,
I prefer valentines
with exotic postmarks,

serrated edges.
Don't worry, Sailor,
I was meant for Carolina.

But you should know
I leave a wake
without a vanishing point.

I refuse to shake the sea
salt from my hair.

Just Another Aviary

Hands are drawn
to you like the first crow
to the scarecrow's arms,
inhibited yet hungry
                    —Jason Stipp

I'm a crow, then,
and there is reason to be afraid.
A broom-handle backbone
with arms thrown open in measures,
you gather starlings to your clef,
tease cornstalks with yellow
and black flannel, tickle their tassels.
You offer little resistance to wind.
Here you are in the ground—this bar,
those starlings—and I'm a rook
with a preened ponytail, ebony
feathers. Vinyl and patent leather.
Your forearms twitch
with straw, broken needles
under your cuffs as you labor
with liquor, the promise
of a hard red. Kerchief,
you're every Main Street
coated with afterglow until I glisten,
pick insects from your mouth,

spin you inside out, murmuration
reduced to blackberries. I take a sip,
continue to stitch my name
into your collar, my eyes
still sharp as my beak.

Scarlett Johansson's Pink Panties

Make me want to touch her,
curled on a windowsill like a cat,
trapped in a minaret of modern

efficiency, glass. Knees scraped
nascent, pale and faulty.
Hanes Her Way, those panties,

cotton, quotidian. Nubility
moved past lingerie
and love songs, the kind that never

believed in garters in the first place.
Intimacy rooted in backyards,
the empty toilet paper tube.

It's not plot that makes me
wish her head under mine.
Once, on my way to Prague,

I met an Army private named
Rick who held my hand all night
over cobblestones so I wouldn't fall.

I didn't.
Or running with Lara,
her black, curly bun a compass

rose among drugstores in Paris.
That duck, duck, goose
a trail of corkscrews and tendrils

until we made the Metro,
sprinting in patent leather.
Yes, abandon can be practiced.

Those kind of nights,
Scarlett, your pink wig
like a bottlecap I once caught

in my bra and kept for luck
under my pillow,
waiting for you to happen again.

Where You Touched

The dance
where you touched
my hips, wouldn't
look at me.
Wrists on your neck
collaring your sweater,
skin fingernails away.
I take your friends'
glances and throw
them back, catfish
too small to keep.
My eyes shut inside.
Streamers tangle
above us. Someday,
I'll mail you my braces.
As if your hands
palms flat and ironed
have a right
against the hem of my skirt.
Your profile
lace in my slip.

On Hearing a Poem by a 12-Year-Old Girl

How brave children are. Half-
lings who can't see the bottom,
sentient and swearing.
One foot in and already cold.
Little, little girl.
My side of the moon
looks dark and vast
and yours still fragrant
with fingerprints of celandine,
hollyhock. Blind spots never heal,
no matter how mirrors tilt.
I would fix them for you,
I swear by the pregnancy of apples.

You said:
I said to they—
Oh, yes, I will.
Be wary. Suddenly,
you are sickled, a pickpocket.
In love with larceny,
the rhythm of your own rape.
Why choose hypotenuse?
Slant over straight, grace
notes over trill? Why
take cream and sugar?

As if identity lies in picnics,
potato salad. Love is no
game of fetch, and walls
waver with sympathetic resonance.

I say: Love your larynx
with coconut butter, violets.
Eat sex wax, honeycomb.
Your inamorata half siren,
half catcall. The spinning house
will know who sent you.
Do this for me.
Refuse their lighter,
that laryngeal ratchet.
When your tracheostomy is choked
with bath salts, rosemary,
they'll cut off your hands.
Say to them:
Bury my limbs,
leave my voice.
I said to they.
Baby, good for you.

WICHITA

My mother riveting—
at the Boeing plant on Oliver,
gunning metal into metal.
Did she smack gum to pass time?
Juicy Fruit, Teaberry—trying
to recall Del Shannon lyrics,
her tan cowboy boots pointing
upward, predetermination
in each loop stitch.
I bet she took smoke breaks
without one lipsticked cigarette.
She only knew first names—
Peg, Debra, Evelyn.
Was it Peggy beside her
when the hydraulics failed,
and the machinist came?
Did her boots catch his eye,
or the strain of her jeans tight-
lipped under her sweater? Maybe
he liked to imagine her
gum falling to the ground.
Or was it later, in the gravel
lot out back, when he watched her
throw a leg over the motorcycle,
hair tossed up like wheat chaff?

What a kick-start.
She must've revved the engine,
her ankles turning over
as he called her name.

Red Dress Cento #3

My mother left in a white dress
and came home in a red dress.
My sister was standing outside
in a bright red dress
clapping her hands.

If love is a red dress,
I am a red dress.
The red dress my mother tore
when my father dipped her.

He was a man for every woman
who dared to wear a red dress.
She was sleek in a red dress with red
pumps, the boys with slick hair, tight jeans.

The first picture is her all sass and flash in a red dress.
Shadows, the skin of them, were ice cubes that flashed
from the red dress to the roof. She thinks about a hard rain,
answering his call in a red dress. When her whole life is full

of risks, the little red dress will always seem right.
She'll know soon enough a red dress will never save her,
the girl in the red dress hating the red dress.
I imagine her like this,

not a strained red dress with tape on her heels,
in the red dress I wear to her funeral.
The sky moving much too quickly,
a red dress and a shoe flying by.

The heat and that damned red dress of hers.

Deus ex machina

Baryshnikov kicks back
on the seat of a Harley Softail,
bare feet splayed over
handlebars, frayed blue jeans
and each toe like an upturned
typewriter key. Pushed,
his toes strike so hard
London screams and lampshades
wobble as if the moon
turned sunny-side up. Tides
reverse. The cuffs of an Oxford
shirt flap about his wrists,
letting the tips of his forearms,
latent obscenities, sniff the air,
reminding women everywhere
of the power of retraction.
They wince, these women,
skittish with compunction
from looking past the fence.
Scarecrows who need polishing:
embrocation by fingertip
across spine, lacquer over
ivory, somatic vigilance.
We all should be so tended.
Valued as an armillary sphere

of well-inhibited brass,
an aged double-malt,
or stairs ministered with wax
and stripped to velvet from use.

Love Song for Billy Pilgrim

Listen:
We all turn to pumpkins at midnight.
When music is reduced to violet light
and hum, we give ourselves over to garden.
So it goes.
The song's prelude is a girl who levitates.
Four boys drink beer behind her,
brown bottles in absent-minded vibrato,
the perihelion of table and hip
a lingering pulse in the station's desolation.
A bell rings in the distance.
She stares at the schedule—its reds,
blacks and yellows. Tiny vixen,
colors that seduce with repetition:
Ankunft, ankunft,
coming coming coming.
How soothing,
the familiarity of numbers, lists
straight down like steel beams, tracks.
She aches for the implicit motion
found in fives, nines, the button-
candy colons that satiate,
utilitarian, sweet, infinity
spooled into eights.
Her thumbs warm burrows,

her shirt that runs
to her hips, lies like sugar.
Syncopated from ankle to lip,
she seethes with lotus, acorn,
the need to be filled with babies.
A bell rings in the distance.
Somewhere in the bridge, I talk to Billy.
Explain in pedal tones that
this is not the how or why,
the explanation for amber.
This is your nap in the wagon, Billy,
green and coffin-shaped.
My tequila, my Puerto Rico,
my Fourth of July.
Anticipation licks her neck,
thick and weighted as salt,
and she begins to swell with numbers:
Five, five, five-o-five. Nine ten. Nine twenty-five.
Eighteighteighteighteight.
Their laughter a bull
in the bottoms of her sixes,
a slump against her sevens.
A blackbody spectrum, she is enlightened,
nirvana. Love made through the window,
and their bottles meant for the blood
gutter of her back. Amazing, the fit.
This is it. Communion
living in air, waiting
for open mouths. Wind
connecting souls at will.
Water and wafers.
The song's coda is a girl who levitates,
chooses silver boots
over glass slippers,
melts wafers.

I promise you nothing but wind.
Water and sunshine's serendipity.
Holy, holy, holy.
It will come again.
In the form of a coffin,
green and wagon-shaped.
You pick:
Diamond?
Denture?

AGNOSTIC

I was in love with her then.
All daisies and dancing.
At night sometimes,

she'd run around our room
in blue cotton underwear,
shrieking like metal.

Unformed legs of tallow
hanging from wicks.
She'd push her nose up,

nostrils pink and ornery,
snorting like a pig
until I peed.

That kind of friend.
Then she got religion—
began to count my sins

on her headboard.
Never even baptized,
I drink tequila limeless,

stomp my feet on the bar,
kiss boys on the mouth.
Sometimes, I wear stockings.

Heels that make my calves
ripe as peapods,
or occasionally curse—

big abrasive sounds,
manholes where steam escapes.
I sleep in on Sundays.

But once, I carried her home.
Wiped lunch from her shirt,
washed smoke from her hair.

She Asks About Africa

Again? He says.

Tell me about the plains.

> Febrile as your hips, warm
> as toast. My palm flat
> on your stomach. My nose
> soft in your ear.
> Fragile and whirring
> with sorrel, that saffron
> basin, melting honey.

And the birds?

> Machetes slapping leaves.
> Goldenrod, plum, salmon.
> Red as rising heat,
> when they speak
> it's a living room of relatives.

The night.

> No, he says,
> the night is mine.

Tell me about love,
about Georgia.

Yes.
That slow,
spaded earth.

LABRADOR
—for Adam

I still sleep with one arm
tucked under, Heisman

straight. Is this all
we were? Bodies that knew

to keep another warm.
Even the silver bar behind

your teeth had manners.
I remember all the things

I've forgotten about you
although I promised otherwise—

oil on the pillow
like a mongoose, bare feet

in winter. Holes in the crotch
of your jeans but three farms

for my horseshoes. Frozen
eggs and no leftovers.

You walked right out
of your sandals—happiness

a straight line, a goal,
hips wide as a woman's.

How I forgot when we met.
But I can still taste Nat Shermans

on your breath weighted
with Christmas lights and snow,

toenails jack-knifed like treetops.
Did I not see your scratched legs

in bed, the bus pulling away?
My shoulders just wouldn't fit

into your aching,
overgrown hands.

Exodus

Inhaling is good for the lungs,
so I do it—swallow your words
tight and clean as the rivet's wound.

There's only so much air.
Slow the violin's groan,
that arc from fire to orange,

night to black—flaws
hardening in amber,
lacquered at the throat.

Too much sap,
round bruise-drops.
Our patina greens and waxes.

A tar thicket of grazed knees,
mingled fingers.
My cherry bomb now soot.

My grudges, tiny bludgeons
I carry in my purse, hide
under my fingernails.

Where is your pocketknife,
your flail?
Inhaling, I bleed.

Out my wrists, my ears,
my eyes. A sudden loosening,
slippage. The great drain,

this exodus.
Exhaling, I return the favor,
blow fact back in your mouth.

DRIVING AT TWILIGHT

I pretend I'm in New Mexico,
gripping handlebars on highway
silver with cholla and barbed wire,

the hot tick of metal between my legs.
A guitar shimmies, steel bleeding
from Sante Fe that won't let

all the beauty out, and what anguish
it is to keep it in. A slow desert
wind through the contrail

and Chris Cornell on the radio—
his voice an eclipse
tripping over gearshifts,

salvation and orgasm
a well-oiled Kawasaki
down Forty near Gallup

with Chris' face in my hair
and everything
coated in dust, life beating us

like graupel that hurts nowhere
all over. I won't make sunrise—
I've become coyote

melon and shrapnel. Friendly fire,
the rimmed arches of his boots
cutting teeth on my heels.

The Valentine Factory

Mother, I must admit I blame you
for giving until nothing remains—

construction paper whose center
has been cut into the shape of a heart

and removed. You're left with outline,
a grudge against scissors.

I try to live for us both
and fail, greedy for duplication—

the only way I know how to hold
my own scissors (orange-handled, left-

handed) so heart after heart blooms
into its own replica, connected

at the edges, so many red streamers.
A valentine factory

based on the prototype
you gave me, the copyright,

the family business.

NOTES

- After Reading Fennelly's *Open House* — is for Jessi Lee.

- Just Another Aviary—Epigraph is from *Clavicle* by Jason Stipp.

- Labrador—is after Mary Biddinger. "Formula of my happiness: a yes, a no, a straight line, a goal" is Nietzsche.

- Looking for Desnos—Refers to Nick Flynn's poem *Angelization*. "Angelization" is what Flynn refers to as "the process by which technology disembodies us."

- Meditations on a Ball Bearing—is after Yusef Komunyakaa.

- Poem for Jason Ray—is after Jenn Morea after Simone Muench. "The language between them, the hidden" is by Jenn Morea.

- Put Your Hands on the Plow and Hold On— is for Ed Roberson.

- Red Dress Cento #1—Thanks to the following authors: Kristy Bowen, "Mr. Godey's Latin"; Anna Camilleri, "Sounds Siren Red"; Nicholas Cobic; Catherine Daly, "Scarlet"; Mary Fell, "Chinatown, 1873"; Ron Koertge, "Fever"; Duane Locke, "'The Poem Is an Answer to a Question or Questions No One, Including the Poet, Had Thought to Ask' Ann Lauterbach 'Slaves of Fashion'"; Sarah Manguso, "Wild Goose Chase"; Orlando Ricardo Menes, "Abuela Nena"; Simone Muench, "Red Dress"; Josie Raney, "Sluts"; Rainer Maria Rilke, "Child in Red"; Anne Sexton, "Killing the Love"; Brenda Shaughnessy, "Your One Good Dress"; and Edith Südergran, trans. David McDuff, "On Foot I Had to Cross the Solar System."

- Red Dress Cento #2—Thanks to the following authors: Aaron Anstett, "Tell Me"; Mary Jo Bang, "Don't Know Why There's No Sun Up in the Sky Stormy Weather"; Julia Bloch, "I Dream I'm the Death of Buffy the Vampire Slayer"; Yves Bonnefoy, trans. Hoyt Rogers, "Let This World Endure"; Lucille Clifton, "to my last period"; Peter Covino, "Poverty of Language"; Steve Earle, Sheryl Crow, "Go Amanda"; John Findura, "Pining To Be Human"; Beatrice Hawley, "Remedies"; Kristin Kelly, "Love Story"; Dorianne Laux, "Antilamentation"; Carol Muske-Dukes, "Field Trip"; John J. Trause, "Daughters of the Revolution"; Ed

Volker, "Back to Loveland"; and Tom Waits, "Red Shoes by the Drugstore."

- Red Dress Cento #3—Thanks to the following authors: Kelli Russell Agodon, "Picking Cherries"; Erin Belieu, "In the Red Dress I Wear to Your Funeral"; Anna Camilleri, *I Am a Red Dress*; Martin Espada, "Now the Dead Will Dance the Mambo"; Joy Harjo, "Deer Dancer"; Tim Kahl, "Vitalis"; Stellasue Lee, "Ah Men"; Victor Lodato, "Edith's Trailer"; Sheryl Luna, "Bones"; Maria McKee, "If Love Is a Red Dress (Hang Me in Rags)"; Melissa Montanez, "Bee Stung"; Simone Muench, "Red Dress"; Rainer Maria Rilke, "Child in Red"; Anne Sexton, "The Red Dance"; Cole Swensen, "The Day They Brought the Radio Home"; and Wayne H. W. Wolfson, "Verse Chorus Verse."

- Two Kinds of Arson—"Girl gone up like a match" is from *Pyromancy* by Ellen Wehle.

- Where You Touched—is for Kevin Lindblom.

Acknowledgments

Some of these poems have appeared in or are forthcoming from (sometimes with different titles or in different versions) the following publications: *After Hours, Another Chicago Magazine, Barn Owl Review, Barrelhouse, Born Magazine, Cider Press Review, Columbia Poetry Review, CutBank, DIAGRAM, Eclipse, Eleventh Muse, Flyway, Fugue, Georgetown Review, Icon, Iowa Writes, Keep Going, Licking River Review, MiPOesias, Natural Bridge, North American Review, Pacific Coast Journal, pacificRE-VIEW, Pebble Lake Review, PERMAfrost, Poetry in the Round, Reservoir, Salt Hill, Seven Corners, South Carolina Review, Sow's Ear Poetry Review, Spindrift, Steam Ticket, Touchstone, Wicked Alice,* and *Yemassee.*

Several of these poems also are featured in a chapbook, *Two Kinds of Arson* (dancing girl press, 2007). "Driving at Twilight," "Garden Run Wild," "Like the Devil," "Nostalgie de la boue," and "Origins" are featured in the chapbook *Impossible Poses* (Switchback Books, 2007). "Meditations on a Ball Bearing" was nominated for a Pushcart Prize in 2006 by the *North American Review.*

Sincere thanks go to my family and friends, Angie Homan, Maryann Homan, Erin and Devon Ingle, Dixie Finger, Kristy and Travis Stewart, Kristen Chamberlain, Beth and Brandon Meier, MaryAnne Lyons, Garrett Brown, David Trinidad, Joan Larkin, Hanna Andrews, Becca Klaver, Andrew Trebing, Michael Robins, Kristy Bowen, Ed Roberson, Arielle Greenberg, Crystal Williams, Mackenzie Carignan, Steven Kovach, Vince Gotera, Grant Tracey, Connie Mogard, Ursula Sokolowska, Columbia College Chicago, the Ragdale Foundation, the Switchback Books women, the Chicago poetry gals, the editors who have published my work, the poetry blogging community, and everyone else who has been patient along the way. Especially to Tony Frazer and Shearsman Books. I am eternally grateful.

Also to Jessi Lee Gaylord—may you always be Kim Addonizio to my Dorianne Laux—and to Mary Biddinger and Simone Muench, who are forever my heroes.